MACRo
MICRo
ATOMIC

MACRO
MICRO
ATOMIC

Poems by
Camille Ora-Nicole

Macro Micro Atomic
© 2023, Camille Ora-Nicole
ISBN: 979-8-2182829-4-3

First Edition, 2023
Orange Chrysanthemum Publishing

Printed in the United States of America

Edited by Megan Giddings
Reviewed by Sondra Rose Marie
Cover Design by Camille Ora-Nicole
Layout Design by Amy Garbin

This book is dedicated to my family and ancestors, my wife, and every teacher that ever encouraged me to write.

And, thank you so much to the Community Literature Initiative (CLI) for inspiring me, teaching me, and providing guidance in putting all my scribbles in one place.

CONTENTS

SECTION TWO: MICRO

SECTION THREE: ATOMIC

PREFACE

This book of poetry is about acknowledging where you came from, accepting the strengths and flaws that are inherited, and finding a way to use that unique set of traits and lineage to forge a path forward. This book is for the black folks, the queerdos, the ones trying to make peace with childhood traumas, those looking for love, and those trying to make magic in a broken world.

MACRO

MICRO

ATOMIC

Section One:

MACRO

Prayers to Mother 1:3

If god is creation,
then you are the ocean
and I praise you
in all your power and majesty.

You are perfect,
so of course we pour our filth
in you; if a human is capable
of one thing, it's to ruin a good thing.

Mother, you don't give what we can handle
You give back what we give to you.

I pray for your mercy.

//

Camille Ora-Nicole

History 1:3

Where is my history?
Where are my roots?
They can't be as shallow
as Southern charmed
magnolias on my skin,

but they don't test ancestry for free,
so this land is all I know.
For hundreds of years,
Mississippi mud, Louisiana mud,
is where I'm from.

Have you ever looked at mud?
It sparkles, it's marvelous.

//

History 2:3

I have my shotgun house.
I have my dreams of warmth,
fire contained in a grill.
I have my hopes past a shotgun,
past a gun, past police state,
past roaming uniforms.

(Don't you know uniforms only mask bad behavior?
I should know—I went to parochial schools.)

I have my oceans, I have my hair
nappy in the salt. I have my stars
and cigarette ash like stars,
the galaxy on Sunset.

I have a park, and a pool where
the faith of a mustard seed made me
feel like magic and where
broken words tempted me
to drown in the waves
my faith made.

I have the earth under my fingernails
and the fruits of the earth in the kitchen
and the fruits of the womb as my family fills
rooms without enough doors and no locks
and plenty of pickles.

I have a family to support me
and family to distress me
and family anxiety to live alone with;
god doesn't help much.

Camille Ora-Nicole

I have exposure, love, heartbreak, lights in tunnels, all
in the heart of Los Angeles, all the gems in
forgotten corners. Family even in the worst
messes, friends even in the saddest hours.
Food when I'm hungry, a blanket when I'm cold,
a notebook when inspired, a pillow when I'm tired.

I have that—

//

History 3:3

I have a history, we have
a history, whether long or short
or a mixture of both

(a mixture of both, I think).

I have an aesthetic, we have an aesthetic
stolen, hidden, recovered, killed, muddied.

But didn't I say mud
was marvelous?
It sparkles, it's magical,
you put mud on our names

and we grow something Else.

//

Camille Ora-Nicole

For I Have That

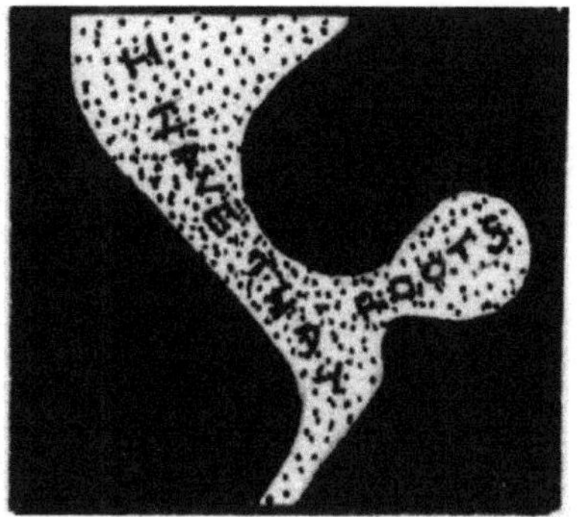

Fro 1:3

He likes my fro.

He doesn't know it's me allowing myself to be lazy.
Letting my hair be free, a concept only
recently grasped by white minds,
stunned by hair strands that
can stand tall all on their own.

People so often fear what they don't know.
I am no different, so I add to what I know everyday.

Here is what I know:

I know how breakfast stove hot asphalt feels under my feet.
I know how a seagull's sharp looks are indicative of sharper
actions.

I know how salt-filled air feels in my nostrils,
can feel the grit in sudsy seawater.

I know the stares as I walk as carefree as my hair
in places that never expected me,
as I hold my own against cheese graters,
my skin only ever slightly bruised.

//

Fro 2:3

I was raised to press my hair
to fit in with Palos Verdes,
impress church folx with visions of
black excellence in a place where
gen. pop. definition of black excellence
is proximity to whiteness.

Other than being followed in stores and
urged to play sports, given
sympathetic nods for living in the ghetto,
I got away unmutilated, unbeaten, just
a little paranoid, with cat-scratch tracks
playing on my skin as reminders of
microaggressive remarks mislabeled
as compliments or curiosity or love.

I wish I didn't have to underplay
aggression to protect my heart.
I wish I was never obliged to
threaten my own head.

//

Fro 3:3

I stopped threatening my ears with hot combs
burning my scalp with perm,
forcing my hair to be everything it wasn't.
I told my hair I loved it, moisturized it,
grew it, twisted it, fro'd it, puffed it,
let it tell me what it wanted to do instead of
punishing it for being what it is,
stuffing it in a box where it doesn't fit,
let it take up room.

Let myself take up room,
let my skin color a room,
let my words charge the air,
let my smile exist,
let my joy exist,
in ways no one knew was possible.

Let my anger prowl,
let my tears flow,
let my eyes close with exhaustion,
let my fingers fiddle nervously,
let my anxieties show.

I show my textures.
They proved me to be human after all.

//

Camille Ora-Nicole

For Fro

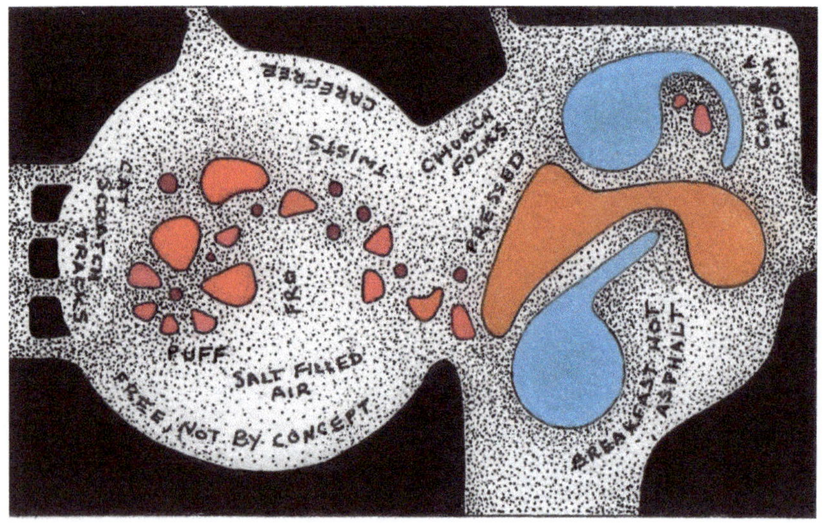

Feels 1:4

How does Beverly Hills feel? What is the nature of the looks
you get? Or do you not bother to notice—because if you
do, you'll find that eyes can be bullets . . . no matter whether
they're Black Lives Matter or All Lives Matter (ew), the eyes
are bullets. Maybe you're sick of the bullets. But you cover
yourself in the warm protection of "I don't give a fuck," which,
coincidentally, looks like wearing sweatpants to Gelsons
while everyone else wears lululemon, grabbing your over-
priced coconut water and organic peanut butter while ignor-
ing the eyes that are actually bullets, and heading back to the
painting they've decided you belong in.

//

Feels 2:4

How does Malibu feel? A little bit like heaven, with PCH being purgatory. I don't belong there, really, but I don't care, really. No one owns the sea, and my skin pairs nicely with the faded beachfront homes following the curves of the hillside. No one owns nature, not really. No matter how hard anyone tries, the air will caress or slap me the same as the next person. The water's temperature doesn't change around anyone, not unless you piss in it. The sun kisses everyone just the same. The sand takes your footprints and mine. The horizon is out of reach of every arm. No one owns nature. No one owns the coast; I don't care what any deed says. We are all just wor-shippers of the sea, the atmosphere playing as the church's dome.

//

Feels 3:4

How does Los Angeles feel? Los Angeles feels like dirt and diamonds, desperation and **pain** and joy and freedom and pain. You can almost feel the gravel in your mouth as the sun makes the buildings shine like diamonds. Los Angeles is a constant push and pull. Los Angeles is not my home, but it is my home. It is a gilded cage, but with so much to see that sometimes it's hard to see the bars. It would be easy to stay caged, unless the words of Octavia Butler come true and even the bars burn away. Even knowing what I know, I would mourn a city with so much texture that the very air is solid against my fingertips.

//

Feels 4:4

How does Compton feel? Compton feels like red dirt from the baseball field near the 1003 house, and sounds like bounce castles and kids on bikes. It smells like rain and other sweet things, even as everyone sweats to make ends meet, one way or another. It tastes like red #40 and watermelon and chicken and tajín, and corn. It tastes like ice cream and strawberries and collard greens and beans, and a desperation to see dreams play out. Compton is country as fuck, and as urban as urban gets. Compton doesn't just feel like home, like a warm blanket. Compton is home.

//

For Feels

GILDED CAGE
SWEET RAIN
DREAM COUNTRY
PAIN
HOME
WATERMELON TAJIN
FINGER TITS
BALLER
PURGATORY
PEANUT BUTTER

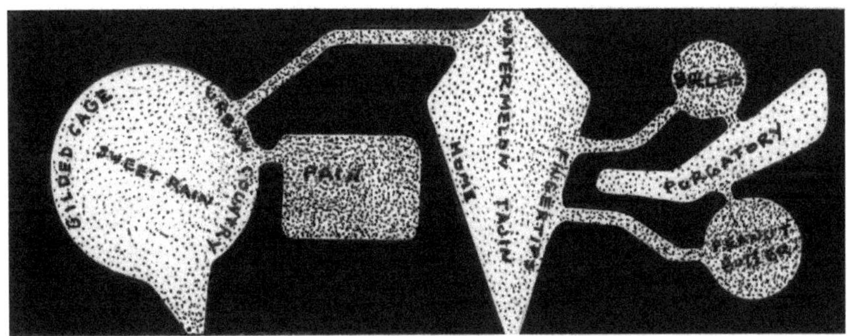

Camille Ora-Nicole

Odd Skin

We used to mourn odd skin, odd heart,
Death 'round a whisper in an ear
Chance encounters, looks that linger
Just a lil too long (a lil too long).
Hands held by friends just a lil too long.
Pause on that channel just a lil too long.
Know just a little too much (too much),
know just a little too much.

We used to mourn, our magic covered in dust
Dyed with blood, threatened
By an inability to rise,
Inability to find love and really revel in it.

That table has turned, hasn't it?
(Thank fuck). We stopped believing
All we had was hidden love,
We threw bricks and built institutions
Just for us.

(Wanna know a secret? The gay agenda is
Breaking chains and spreading love and
Sipping iced coffee and smirking
In the face of cisheteronormativity.
It's consent and sexy tings and I'll let
You be if you let me be but since
The world won't, it'll have to look at me.
I'm going nowhere til you look at me.)

The records are going again
As they have for centuries.
Time to dance, again, from dusk til dawn,
Revel in the future we got.
Honor the past from which we were begot.

Atlas

They don't see you, holding up their pedestals,
like Atlas holding up the world.

The world is shaped by men on pedestals,
beholden to themselves, too stupid to look down.

Ignorant to you, blind to the cosmos
that shines in your eyes;
a sight that speaks truth to the
inverse universe they float in.

You are the dark matter.
You are the light.

You are explosions and their emerging patterns.
You are creation itself.

A swirling mass of genius,
the electric spark behind the gears.
You're not a god, you are not perfect;
You're not a void, only voids are perfect,

But you are more than they see.
And they won't see until they topple.

//

Camille Ora-Nicole

Blue/Pink

Didn't I tell you
LA was blue?
Bluer than my heart
on a rainy day.

There's something beautiful
about struggle.
The deepest blues bloom
into the sweetest pinks
(if you survive, that is).

I believe in you, LA,
my sanctuary city.
I'm here for you
throughout your gradient—

//

Paradise Lost

It's hard to call home paradise
when your home is on fire;
when train conductors instruct
you to look for damage like we're
looking for Easter eggs
at a fucked up Disneyland.

I want to stay loyal to my queen
CALIFIA, as called thanks to the Moors,

but I can't breathe,
I can't see.
The ash is suffocating;
if only we had known—

Maybe we would have left this
sun-drenched paradise, this
island on the land,

alone.

//

Camille Ora-Nicole

To The Blond Girl

To the girl with the blond hair
and the blue eyes: I envy you.

I don't envy
your blond hair, or your blue eyes;
I like my zigs and browns just fine.
I envy your ability to ignore the insanity
of inequality sitting right beside you.

Blond girl with blue eyes,
You never have to hide.
Your family's pride is getting by;
my family's pride is we're alive.
We haven't died.
We managed to rise,
yeast-free,
we've captured snatches of dreams,
tasted notes of cream.

Girl with blue eyes, blond hair,
you get to be unaware,
if you so choose,
of how bad it can feel to lose
when you're not white in a
white-is-supreme country
And girl, I do,

I envy you.
I prefer my zigs and browns,
but I sure do envy you.

//

Fickle Femininity

We were always too soft,
always too old,
never hard enough
never old enough.

We were never enough,
doomed to never be enough,
doomed to be ground like dust
under the boot
of the most taciturn creature:

HuMans.
With all their fragility
and ill-placed egos.

HuMans,
with their constant
need for air
and casual game of turntables,
turning the tables
on bedrooms, homes,
cities, states, entire nations,
for one girl.

A girl that should be soft
but also hard.
A girl that should be dumb
but also play her card.
A girl that should grow up
to always seek youth.
A girl that should never reach up
from the lower deck
and instead enjoy the partial view.

//

Camille Ora-Nicole

Keep Hoping

The future will be the past.
Where will we be in ten years?
Will we ask acquaintances
if they've felt the sun lately?
Risked burns from an ozone-free star
To feel warmth, then weep?

Is it too late to dream?
Or is it safer to settle for apartments
and pray for mercy from our lords,
(our landlords)

I don't want to say we're fucked
(even if we are),

Because I want us to keep dreaming
I want us to keep hoping.

//

Bless These Hands, American Damned

Bless these hands, American damned
Dipped in blood and dried with sand
Blue black veins from wrist to fingers
This flag it lingers, this curse, this cancer.

Bless these hands, American damned
Breaking hammers with sharp sickles
No rest for the weary, grabbing shovels
To bury the falsehoods of this land.

Bless these hands, American damned
Forsaking the hood and sweet nepenthe
For dreams of chariots in the sky
Life as sacrifice to a fucked Most High.

Bless these hands, American damned
Pray they get rest before they're dead
Pray they get to nurture dreams
Made technicolor from sacred sleep.

//

Camille Ora-Nicole

red wagons and red strawberries

We used to play
with our neighbors, sharing
red wagons and red strawberries.

We couldn't speak
directly with each other.
That's what Johnny was for.
Translating the Germanic
to the Romantic and back again.

We never went far,
just our yard up to
our steps and to the sidewalk.
But we did so
from noon to dusk.

We had this trust
even as my grandmother
never did,
that little girls offering
strawberries and imagination
couldn't possibly be any
more dangerous than
grass dripping dew in the morning.

//

For red wagons and red strawberries

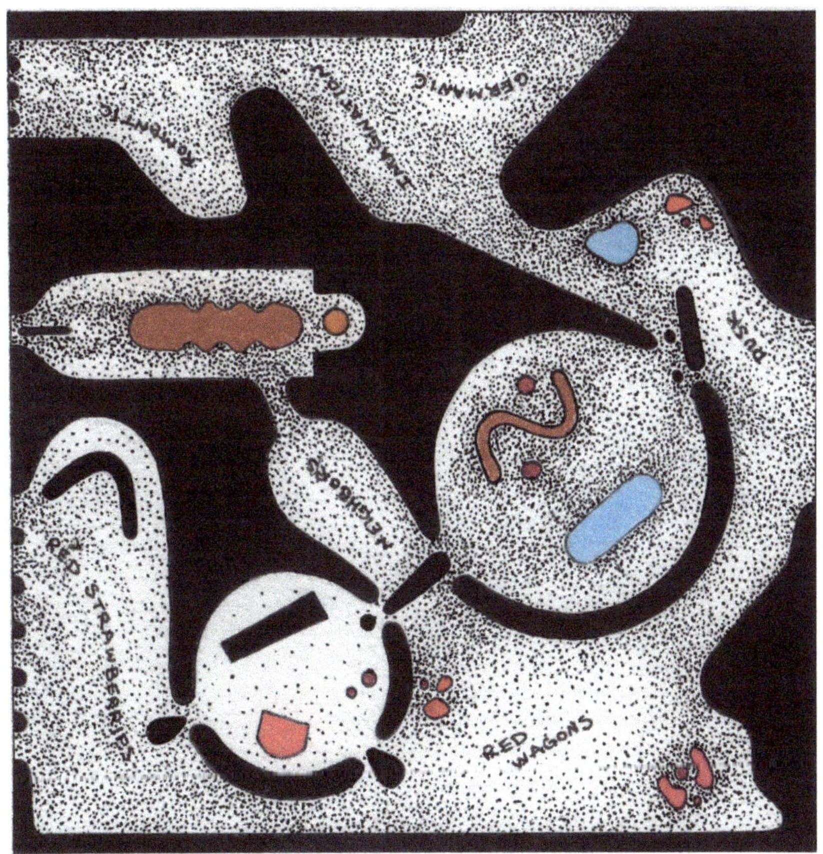

Ivy

How does the ivy grow on the side of the freeway? How is it possible for such greenery to thrive on smog and stress and rocks and hard places?

Have you met ivy? She's stunning, luminescent alien green, nothing that should be feasible on this planet we've ruined, and yet here she is. I wish I was more like her. Resilient. People expect it because my skin is brown and my eyes are brown and my hair is brown—my top crust must be as tough as earth herself, but I crumble under pressure, like dust, like anyone else. Water from my tears holds me up and not much else.

I do know girls like ivy. Or at least I think I do. Maybe they are more like me, and less like the tendrils that are the only thing holding the walls of our speed traps together, keeping us from driving off man-made cliffs and attacking the masses with our ill-directed rage.

//

2024

I am not looking forward to you,
wide-shouldered, teeth white as the cliffs
of a country the forefathers risked death
to emancipate from.
I am not looking forward to you,
and your lies, poor excuses for promises,
gaslighting for an ink-filled bubble
good as a signature on our death certificates.
I am not looking forward to you,
but I do have hope for you.

I am not looking forward to you
as you move into your Oval Office
wherein birthed miracles and war crimes
layers of grime cut through with bleach.
I am not looking forward to you
and your speech of hope, or devastation,
whichever the wind may turn
never satisfying anyone.
I am not looking forward to you,
but I do have hope for you.

I hope you change us for the better.
I hope you heal our hurts.
I hope you prop up the poor of us for once,
and we are all poor except the ones
that bankrolled your campaign.
I hope you smile, take the gain
and run.
Lie to them instead of us.
I am not looking forward to you,
but I do have hope for you.

I hope you make the American dream
everything it should be.
I hope you make the Indigenous whole.
I hope you make the Black folks whole.
I hope reparations sit heavy on your soul.
I hope incarceration prefixes make themselves known.
I hope big corporations quake in your shadow.
I hope we survive Mother's growing tides and blows.

god,
I am not looking forward to you.
Give me one reason to.
But I do have hope for you.
That thing with feathers.

//

Section Two:

MICRo

Prayers to Mother 2:3

Dear Mother,
have I been here before?
sometimes it feels
like I've been here before.

Sometimes the air feels
too familiar.
Sometimes the déjà vu
hits a little too hard.
Sometimes I reach out to you
and it feels like I've
prayed the words I'm saying
before, and again and again and again.
Sometimes unique moments
feel unique only to this moment

Sometimes days feel like dreams
experiencing the passing weeks
as an observer—
waiting patiently for another death—
daresay eagerly for another death.
Death at least is unique, I would think,
and death would lead
to another dream—my mistake,
another life.

Until then Mother, please
have I been here before?
Who was I?

Mother,
Who am I?

Mother,
Who am I supposed to be?

//

Camille Ora-Nicole

Shadow Films

When you were small
and maybe asleep, possibly dreaming,
facing the wall hands clenched
little sister barely sitting up
you, barely out of diapers,
hair barely into barrettes,
you watched a shadow film.
Perhaps your first, or
fighting for first position
with Fantasia and the Little Mermaid.
Bodies were bent in fury,
mouths were wide with words
you couldn't understand.
An arm stretched all the way back,
palm wide open.
You heard a sound like a crack on a soft cheek,
then heard it reciprocated in defense, or
in indignation.
Words didn't yet form in your mind,
your dictionary was still growing
holding you tight.

//

. . . said it'd be okay and it was okay

Youth was moissanite and fool's gold
green grass grown in front of a broken home,
held together with yarn and odds and bits.

It was big breakfasts filling big stomachs
big rooms, floors with cracks
filled with big dreams, big imaginations—
machinations of escape—

Youth was dove calls, rising at dawn
the sun rising over the lemon tree
eternal springs fed greens, daydreams, play scenes, fed me,
fed magic resurrection lilies.

I thought I understood the state of things
but I know nothing.
Were my kindred's sins as bad as they seemed?
Or is my mind just weak,

from gusts and gales of constant feuds,
caught in the middle of pop, hiss, boom,
caught in the middle, waiting for an end
to tense halls and thin walls.

Yarn's not all that strong,
but I huddled in warm blankets,
kept sheltered from the wind as the roof swayed
said it'd be okay and it was okay.

//

Camille Ora-Nicole

Warrior Princess

Set the scene
Late at night (around 8 at night)
Nestled with father and sister
In an iron-ended bed
In a room around the corner and a tree
Away from granny's house
(Father finding independence
In his best friend's mother's house),
We turned on the TV.

Review the TV guide
Find the channel
Adjust the antennas
To clear the screen.
The 90s love static
But not more than I love
A certain cold glare.

Falling asleep
But no dreams for me
Little hands gripping
The bed frame
In eager anticipation
Of her next sword swing,
Her attempt to kill guilt.
She could kill gods
But only death can
Kill her shame.

Fast forward
Years later, stonewalling in therapy
With a soul of icy water
And eyes that won't stop streaming
A throat raw from screams
Unpronounced, falling acidly to a belly
Roiling with waves receding for a tsunami
Broken by a past
That also builds me up.
A past that killed millions
A past that saved millions
A circular sword that
I hate as much as I adore.

//

Camille Ora-Nicole

For Warrior Princess

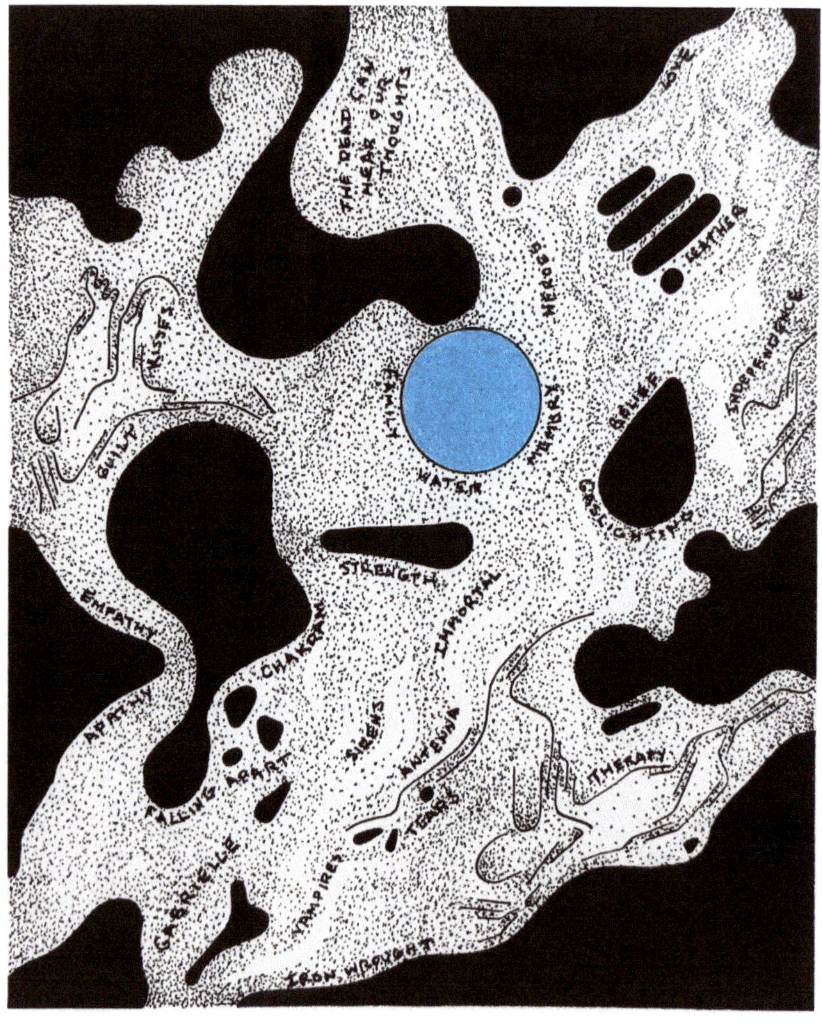

Nintendo

Somewhere behind the screen, the pixels and the colors, the
sounds bit-byted, the ifs and ors,
is a genius I'd like to meet.

I'd like to meet you, genius, and when I say genius I mean
plural,
hive mind behind the Koraidon's glide ability and so much to
see between sea and shining sea.

Sometimes I wish I could be like you, genius, like you, god, like
you, frog under a rock,
musty with ideas and not enough deodorant.

Sometimes I wish I could dream like you, genius, like you, hive
mind, but to see visions like yours
requires multiple brains, similar to how an octopus has
multiple hearts and I have neither.

I need sleep, genius, I need sleep, god. I need sleep, Nintendo,
and I've got none since I was ten.

I need sleep, genius, I need sleep hive mind, I need sleep,
Nintendo,
but I'd never sleep again to be a part of your neuroanatomy.

//

Camille Ora-Nicole

Painted Faces

One summer, hot
as the valley tended to be, we
opened a magic chest filled with
pigments for eyes, lips, cheeks—
colors we were too young to need
but old enough to want.

The girl with the red hair
colored my eyes with blue,
and I hers.
We stood back in pride
admiring our masterpieces.

Masterpieces,
later torn to pieces
by an aunt
who didn't understand
flights of fancies.
She took the color as a mess;
told us to do better.

//

Peanut M&M's

How dare little brother
eat your peanut M&M's!

He's too young, he doesn't
know what you had to do
for those peanut M&M's.
You sacrificed your bliss
for those peanut M&M's
put out your wrists, allowed
the world to slit
to be able to keep an ever-full
jar of peanut M&M's,
precious as fancy chocolates
from Matilda,
an indulgence you deserve.

I remember all those late nights
I sat with you under bright lights
as you did the right thing,
drank from Pierian spring
in the classroom of a university
that didn't mind me
because everyone in that classroom
was doing the same thing.

I remember all those mornings
one bathroom, three young things,
a young thing with young things
30 doesn't mean the same thing
these days. We were swept away
by necessity, mornings turned
to evening, exhausted rise
exhausted sleep but it's worth it, right?

Camille Ora-Nicole

All the things you did
for some peanut M&M's.
A whole slew hiding,
a jar of peanut M&M's.
Necessary distance, to
stop deserving fingers
from devouring peanut M&M's
at a blasphemous rate.
Now you can
afford the peanut M&M's
damn little brother though
making you have to raise
your weary bones
to buy more.

//

For Peanut M&M's

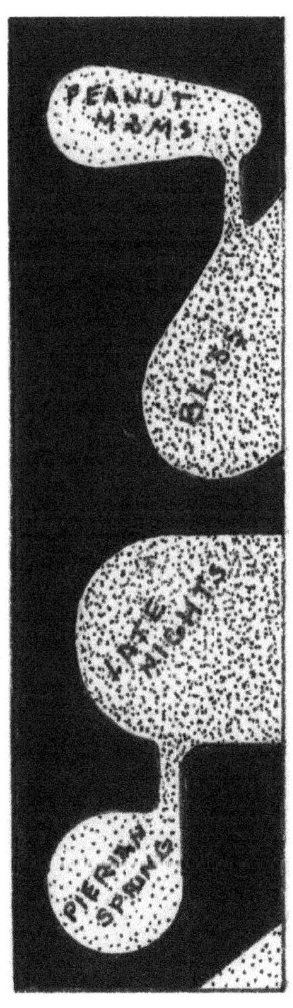

Camille Ora-Nicole

Blockbuster

In the backroom of a Blockbuster
VCR whirring in time
to a blockbuster favorite,
we bided our time

as dad worked his shift
ended unending lines
of people finding their bliss
for a buck ninety-nine.

Meanwhile I grinned over dumb shit:
sticking staples in fingertips
callused from guitar strings
and chanting spells breaking time

chanting spells breaking gravity
once finally outside
could movies be reality?
Or are they illusions, lies

Like a staple in my fingertip
hitting neither blood nor nerve ending
an illusion of long-suffering
in reality numbing?

Could I pretend to be magic
jump off stairwells, Mary Poppins
with umbrella, cinematic
and fly, fantastic?

It'd probably be tragic;
that's why epic is *epic*;
at any number of seconds
the *epic* could *end*.

We drive home instead
of floating amongst the clouds
performing tricks made to look real;
we'll leave it to the reel.

//

Camille Ora-Nicole

Ariel

You'll never know how much you
inspired my particular brand of Drama.

Your line design like lava
creeping towards the sea,
I want to bathe in it,
even if it kills me—

You changed everything by breaking everything
with your deeply disturbing yet jocular soul,
deep underwater with the anglerfish and cockatoo squid.

//

For Ariel

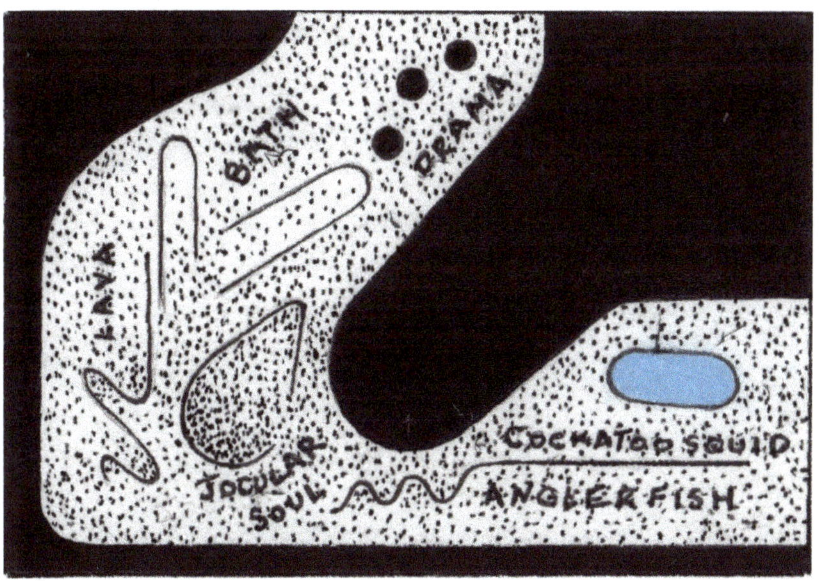

Camille Ora-Nicole

The Traveler

Submerged under a steaming faucet,
I pretended to be a sea traveler
with a submarine helmet just for one.

I spun friendships with creatures
only I could see
as my scalp was scrubbed clean,
suds filling the sink.

I was a mangrove forest
the only separation from the sea
being brown skin, white skull, grey matter—

//

Ora

My granny is gold
like the name she bears
like the soil she toiled,
rich, as she never was
but generous, as she always was,
full of love, cold and sweet.

And spiritually?
She's a yellow kite in a bright sky.

My granny is broken.
Too many doilies woven
with arthritic red wrists.
Too many fists around cushions
absorbing every tear
I never saw.

And her feet?
They've been laid low.

I share her name but not her glow.
Learned her trades, but not her flow
of thought, methodical,
clear in her intentions,
hers a mind of crystal, mine obsidian
absorbing, not reflecting
the Mother's aura.

Could I ever be Ora?
Oh, to be Ora.

//

Camille Ora-Nicole

Mother's Daughter

My mother
is my grandmother's daughter,
rendered lighter
with none of her features
but all of her sins,
all of her weakness,
and all of her strength.

My mother
is a seed grown
in rocky soil,
roots deep, woody stems
keeping the elements at bay.

My mother
has only barely
missed a day,
walked on broken bones
to keep our boat afloat.

I've never seen my mother cry.
I tried to be like her
and my mother's mother,
but my strength isn't
in where they falter;
it's in whenever
they stood strong
through it all.

I am my mother's daughter,
but I am strong enough
to fall apart.
I am strong enough
to cry.
Teacher, Doctor, Lawyer

//

Teacher, Doctor, Lawyer

Teacher, Doctor, Lawyer.
I was raised to be one
but I couldn't get the suit on;
the sleeves were too tight

Teacher, Doctor, Lawyer.
Rolling through Carson,
Subaru lights on;
can't do it, try as I might

Teacher, Doctor, Lawyer.
The really super smart one,
(joke's on them, I'm kinda dumb)
alumni gold star on
shining in the night sky.

Teacher, Doctor, Lawyer.
If I'm a teacher, I'm a bad one.
If I'm a doctor, I'm a green one.
If I'm a lawyer, I'm Better Call Saul.

Teacher, Doctor, Lawyer.
Try artist with a smock on,
protecting clothes from ink blots.
Staring at the sun, waiting for a call,
knowing one might not come at all.

Teacher, Doctor, Lawyer.
Maybe I should have been one.
Maybe I am dumb.
What's true love without foundation?
But then what's true love without love?

//

Camille Ora-Nicole

Tactile

I was looking for something tactile
I remember the tile was always cold so
as anxiety rose like bile to my throat, my cheeks,
I laid my body down as though to sleep.

I heard her pause right outside the bathroom door
I wasn't quiet, I'm sure she heard me moan, but
she kept walking and I learned that day
that emotions didn't matter—best to tuck them away

Instead I kept looking for something tactile
because there was no point in having anything to say
no point in giving emotions a name
if the people you love look away

I still look for the tactile
even though I know it's okay
to say when I'm not okay
parents will fuck you up won't they,

when they unintentionally make tile
your only source of solace
while saying *you're strong, you'll be okay.*

I am as strong as tile today,
and just as easily cracked.
Keeping my pieces together with

omega 3s
therapy
squeezing cats
hugging trees

cuts on fingertips
from metal guitar strings
cuts from paper,
rope burn from yarn
in pursuit of a
pipe dream art career damn near tangible
from comforters providing heat
so tangible it's suffocating,
watching rivulets of sweat
on my arms dance
treasuring every hug
because they feel like acceptance
lips swollen from kisses,
release without shattering,

without tile meeting the head of a hammer,
without feet finding the edge of a cliff
without bleach finding its way down my throat,
without head underwater lungs screaming for drought

stop—

I am so strong until I'm not.

I'd think she'd understand
because I think she's just like me
look there, it's generational, how sweet.

I look just like my mom
except I've started speaking
it's a big step for me
But I think I'll always need something tactile

//

Camille Ora-Nicole

For Tactile

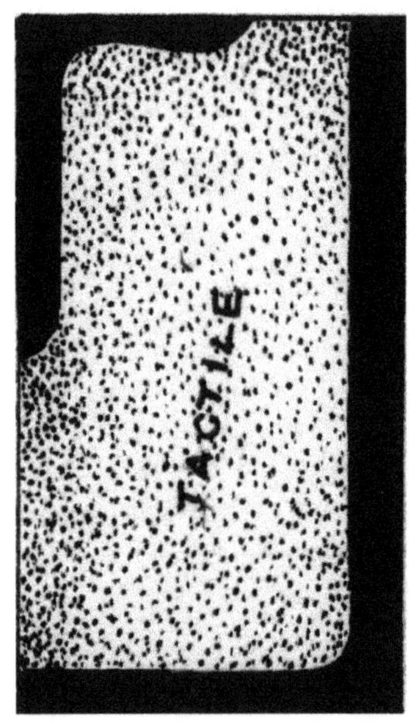

DUO

We needed each other
but you were busy pretending
the sky was always blue;
rocks never fell into the sea.

I needed you
but I was left with dreams,
literary devices, and
forums of sweet strangers.

You needed me
but you struggled alone,
doors closed, no noise
of pain or discomfort.

We need us,
need to share the same sphere
need to share our needs.

We don't need to weep alone.

//

Camille Ora-Nicole

For DUO 3:3

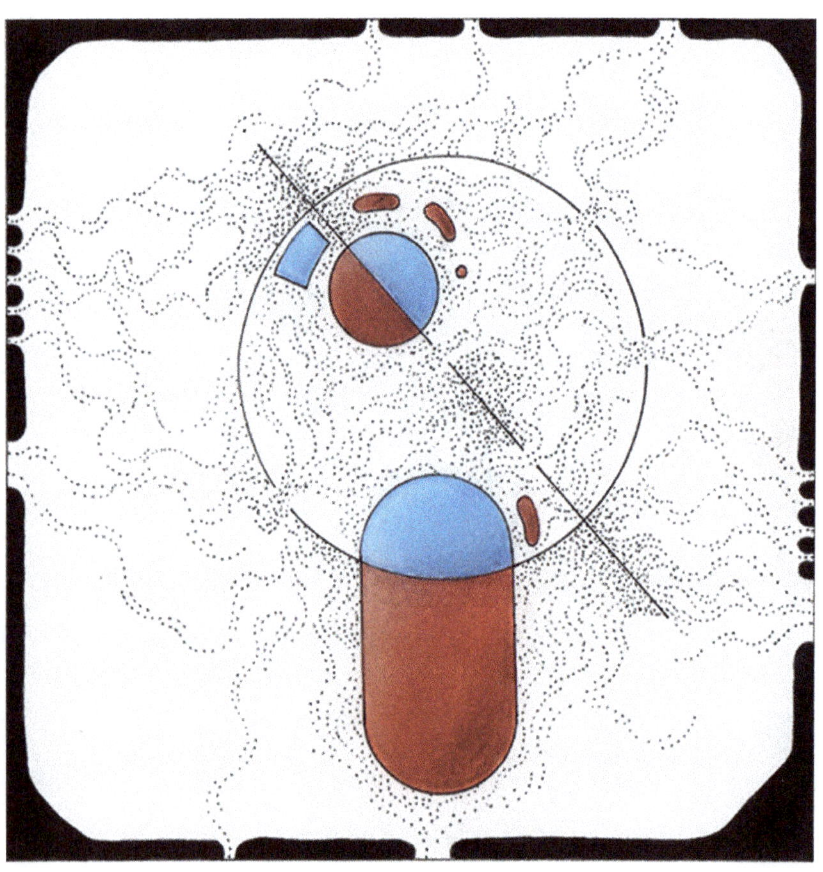

Lilith

So what, she
murmured, hands
dipping low in
water so fresh it
glimmered like sapphires—

So what to
the world in a room
dark and empty, the
gloom her only company, her
thoughts ever-racing—

So what to the work in
that prison called
home, she thought if
she must be alone
then the wilderness was
a better way to go—

Maybe she'd meet the devil
she'd become Lilith–

//

Camille Ora-Nicole

Take Care

Take care.
It's the fair thing
to do in a world
that hates you.

I see you, I see you
I see you, I see you—

I see tendrils of doubt
in hair like witchcraft
cascading down your back,
wrapping around your chest,
choking out any hope that's left.

I see your limbs
held together with pins,
metallic cartilage for a body
that couldn't stop its
mutilation via team salvation
on a grassy field.

I see your heart;
it never healed,
never realized the
blood in its valves
could grow flowers
on its own, a heart that's
only had temporary homes.

I see your eyes, empty,
once gleeful of
a closet full of trophies,
a legacy of insanity,
woefully unseen,
blissfully aware—

Please take care,
you don't want to go there.
Unbend your back
and stand, and stretch,
and wash, and rest.

//

Camille Ora-Nicole

For Take Care

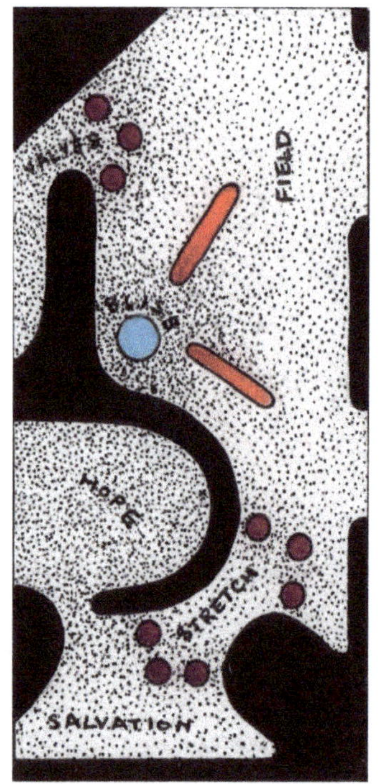

Old and Dying People

I'm not ready to be
old and dying people.
There so much more to see,
more autumn light to drink.
Just another hour,
just one more hour.

It's times like these
I wish I did drugs
almost sober as Callisto.
I wanna let that habit go,
wanna try this habit on.

Damn to be reminded
I won't always see hills,
walk around a park,
drive a car,
be bad at parking.

I used to kill seconds,
now I wish for resurrection.

If the world burns,
I wanna see it burn.
If the desert freezes over,
I'll skate on the ice.
If I lose everyone I love,
I'll find more to call mine.
I'm not done
til I'm done.

I'm not done
til I say I'm done.

//

Camille Ora-Nicole

Coffin Shop

I dunno if I'll survive
You breaking my heart
You might as well buy my coffin while
You're out buying me a tart

Lucky for you there's a coffin store
Down the road, it's shaped like a chapel
Lucky for you there's a chapel
Down the road where you can hold my funeral

Where did you come from?
How did you get here?
Where are you going?
I wanna follow you to the grave

It all started when I looked you in the eye
Your smile wide, Cheshire, it should be a sin
And your voice all around me like a siren
I'm Ulysses and I'm not tied in
I looked to the sky, did a Ginny Wolf,
tied a rock around my ankle
And jumped right in
And everytime I see your light shining above me
I come to life again

Where did you come from?
How did you get here?
Where are you going?
I wanna follow you to the grave

Where did you come from?
How did you get here?
Where are you going?
I wanna follow you to the grave

//

Coffin Shop QR Code

Camille Ora-Nicole

Spirits

Bless nights like magic
Long as the shortest day
In an illegal den
Built by ambitious hands.

Bless TV light breaking
The deep darkness
Throwing light on the spirits
In the corners.

Bless the spirits
I think they may
Be my grandparents
Still watching, always watching.

//

Young Blood

Our family is dying.
Our blood is young now.
Our north stars are fading,
leaving scars on the universe.

I don't want to be alone.
I'm not ready to be alone.
But if I go before you go,
I'm leaving you alone.

My blood survived ships, that's
a feat worth a medal, our feet made it West,
I grew up listening to metal.

My blood survived fields, and
my heart is so rich it's black.
Oil runs in our veins, make a cut and
it'll stain your good name which
wasn't so good in the first place—

(If you have to hide your face, it was ugly in the first place)—

My kinfolks are the shit, even when
they're being shits, I forgive because
I get it, life's been a bitch.

When your blood survives ships
it runs rich, but it'll always be a little sick.
Death lived in those hulls
My rich blood ran down whips.
Tears clung to lips as
my blood hung from trees.
I was bruised when we fell to our knees.

But our blood survived and
Maya was right, they can see it in our eyes.
We can see a glimmer in the mirror
of our immortality, however flawed
in trying to bind us, they made us gods.

//

For Young Blood

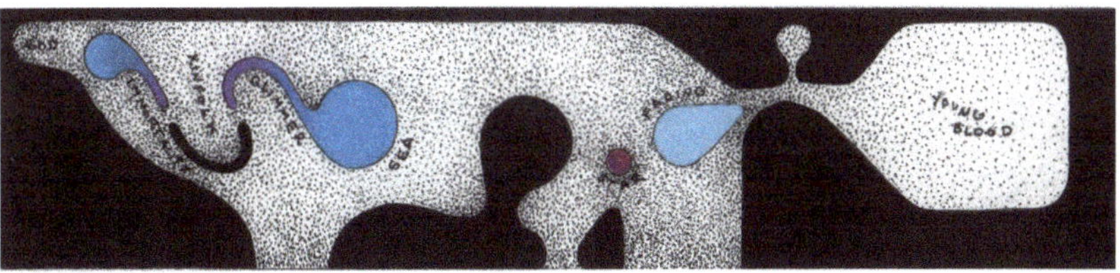

The Night Dances 1:2

The sun rising used to be
all I needed to meet the day.

I could travel the world in one night
and be alright in the morning.

Age both fucks with fun
and makes it more precious.

Dew on a resurrection lily
is the holiest of holies.

//

The Night Dances 2:2

I stood in the middle of that dance floor and experienced heaven—heaven was what everyone called hell, resplendent in its heat, confetti, noise, and freedom.

My friends probably just thought it would be cute—take the underage virgin wearing kitten heels to the club and see what happens. But I was not destined to be a sloppy drunk. Instead I got lost inside the atmosphere.

I stood in the middle of the dance floor and felt. I felt. I felt everything. I felt my soul dance with the music and the lights sparkling on everything it touched. I hugged myself, in love with myself, for the first time in a very long time.

//

Camille Ora-Nicole

Portrait of an Afternoon

Woman
Brown skin gold in the light
Of an open window

Shadow teaching
Monochromatic lessons
On the wall.

Shadows hiding
Half her face from
Technology and therefore
From the world.

Shadows making
Love to light
Pressed up tight
Never letting go.

Enby
Eyes expansive
Restless and full of stars.

Guitar resting
On black pants dense
Enough to eat the world.

Guitar pressing
Under one breast
Sweet flesh covered
In blue-banded cloth.

Guitar raring
To kill the day
With a song
Hallowing heartbreak.

//

Orange Chrysanthemums in the Sand

Is it safe to hold your hand?
Can I try to love again?
Orange chrysanthemums in the sand
My soft heart is delicate

I know I talk a lot on death
But I'm not dead yet
Orange chrysanthemums in the sand

Could I hold your hand
Can I love again
Can we revive again
Can we live again?

Can we depend on each other?
Get through all this life shit together?

Orange chrysanthemums in the sand
Orange chrysanthemums in the sand
Can I hold your hand?
Can I?

//

Section Three:

ATOMIC

Prayers To Mother 3:3

Mother could tell
that we were going to be friends.

There was something in your glance
and a murmur in my soul.

There was shared joy, red.
And shared pain, blue.

There was a question on your lips.
There was a question on my lips.
And we let our questions slip.
And we began to dance.

Our words simply fit,
as did our hands.
Our feet did the right thing,
never guiding us wrong.

And Mother is singing her song,
as we go round and round.
She's never wrong.
I love her song.

//

Camille Ora-Nicole

Her Magic

The sun rises
just to set fire
to her hair.

The ocean exists
just to reflect
on her eyes.

She has magic
in her marrow
where she goes
you cannot follow
and if she goes
so does her glow
then it's nighttime again.

//

Summertime

Summertime had you in it for three years now
and you're leaving now,
the legacy of your presence starting now.
So long now, so long—

It's a muddy feeling, this feeling, of still
Los Angeles hills
without your frantic energy or speech
so long now, so long—

Everyone comes into your life for a reason.
Your season's over
but goddamn, the rains you brought were sweet.
So long now, so long—

I hate to see you go, have I said that?
I don't know.
I tend to speak in between lines,
silent, you can't hear
the melody—I should speak up someday
take a page out of your book—
So long now, so long—

You won't miss the heat,
who would?
You're off to somewhere more green.
I hope life gives you everything

So long now, so long.

//

Camille Ora-Nicole

In Response to Naked in Manhattan

Touch me baby
put your lips on mine—

Would we still be friends if
you put your lips on mine?
If you don't mind I'd like to risk it—
what the fuck am I saying I'd never risk it
unless you risked it first.
I'm giving bottom energy til the end of the fucking world.

Okay here's my logic:
I like how you talk,
how you shape words with your lips
and if I like how you shape words with your lips
I'd think I'd like how you shape kisses with those lips

But you know what I really want?
I want your fingers in my mouth.
I want you to stare me down while I suck them.
Can I say that and still be friends?

Where's the line?
And how far past it can we go
and still be able to backtrack if it all turns into a no-go,
no-fly zone,
God I'm so fucking dumb.

Anyway it's a moot point.
Ultimately this will all go to the back of my mind
as it always does
out of concern for our friendship
(read: out of fear that you'll hate me).
But know that whenever
I listen to Naked in Manhattan, I'm thinking of you.

Touch me baby
put your lips on mine—

//

Camille Ora-Nicole

Praying Mantis

And there it goes—
Noise and lights like a blanket
Sitting in a corner seat
Watching the dancers
Make a blur of the music
Swirling in the air

I saw you
And you
And you
In the bralette
And the short skirt
And the glitter on the cheekbones
And the braids
And the smiles
And the hands that look soft
And the smiles that play soft
Around molly and alcohol—

But I kept missing her
I can't keep her off my mind
All of her hair
And every smile her mouth makes
And every word she says
And her aura
Undiluted by the lights and the noise—

See the lights and the noise
Are a clever veil
Combine it with an overpriced Modelo
And you can think
Love at first sight—
But she don't need a veil
All she had to do was show up one day
And there I was
Caught with no way out
Tragically smitten—

I wish she'd just eat me
Like a praying mantis or some shit
Call it done and over
Call it quits
Instead of leaving me to sit
In a corner booth
In a loud bar
Trying to focus
On what's in front of me
Instead of thinking of
All the ways that she's not here
And all the ways
She rises above everyone—

//

Camille Ora-Nicole

Mutual

i. you dream of tsunamis too.

Scenarios where the entire world
needs to be saved by only you.
Scenarios where brine and refraction
turns the marble blue.
Scenarios where Mother has her victory
and we meet our doom.

Except we survive
and save a couple people too.
Except the sun
doesn't dry our corpses.
Except the sea
only gains a few inches.
Except we flip switches
and become marine animals.
Except the Mother
makes high salt content more edible.

ii. american individualism

You are rarely in my dreams
and never in my tsunamis.
Our imaginary tragedies
are separate, spawning
from anxious real-life existences.
They're hidden in the REM cycle
where no one can witness the effects
of stress on our psyches.

iii. glass half-full

Good thing I love the ocean.
Good thing that the wave is as much
a relief as it is a tragedy.
In reality I don't think I could swim
hard enough to survive a tsunami
What do you think?

Would you simply die too?

//

Camille Ora-Nicole

For Mutual

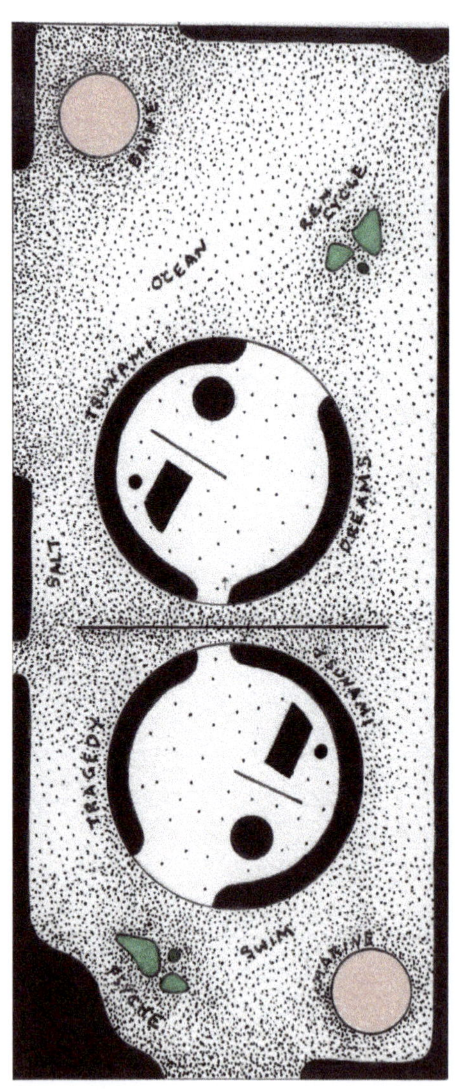

No Seasons

I wasn't looking for her
She appeared laughing
She had a voice so clever
It blew me away
I would have given her everything
I wish that I had

But dreaming and wishing
Don't make love,
They just make songs like this one

While someone else
Is walking the line
Chasing her love in real time
I'm running out of time
I am out of time

And full of excuses like:

She was all light and color
I couldn't say jack shit
At a tree by the water
I could have swept her off her feet

But my mouth wouldn't bother
My feet were unmoving
If she had looked any closer though
She would've seen everything

Camille Ora-Nicole

Green-gold light splashing
On shaking thighs
Her body so close
I'm losing my mind

Now she's off to life under bluer skies
And I just hope she thinks of me sometimes

I never thought
That she would leave
The trees would lose their leaves
Before she left me

California has no seasons
It might if she don't stay
California has no seasons
I don't enjoy the rain
California has no seasons
This desert holds no time
California has no seasons
But time has ended mine.

//

No Seasons QR Code

Camille Ora-Nicole

For No Seasons

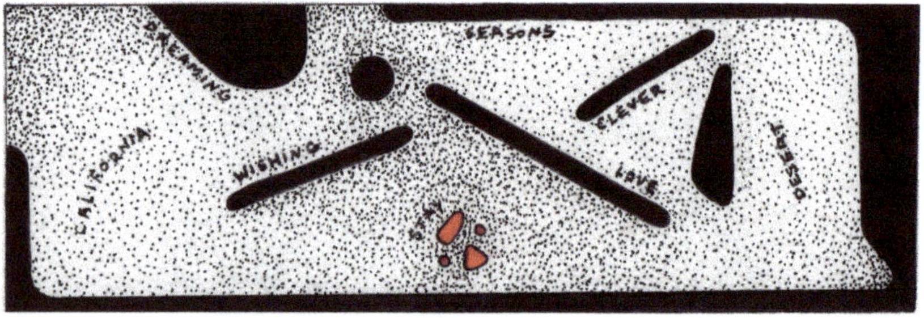

Woo Love

I'll never forget that late July
With sweat in my eyes
I couldn't see what you could see in me
You can't imagine my surprise
When you took me to the side
Sweet as maraschino pie
Told me wait for a second please
Brought coffee with ice
Looked me dead in the eyes
And said it was the last time you'd
Ever ever leave me be
You can make your own choices
I'm glad you're choosing me
But one day I hope you tell me what you had seen

Cuz I know what I'd seen
Our life stretching out before me
You push me off a dead road
I help you carry your load
We help each other realize our wildest dreams
And I don't know what would have been
If you hadn't seen me
And if I didn't open my arms
Disarm all my alarms
And drink that ice coffee

Woo sun
Woo condensation
Woo love
Woo choices
Fuck condemnation
Woo love
Woo chance

Woo fortune favors all the brave
Woo sun
Woo condensation
Woo love

Would mind if I make noise
Blow the lid off your tin house
Kiss the sweat off your brows
As I undo your blouse buttons
Let the sky know we're smitten
That destiny made good choices
It's a match made in heaven
If heaven existed
And if this is hell, it's as fantastic as Dante's
Maybe we'll meet Nas X while we're here
And we've got each other
There's nothing to fear.

Woo sun
Woo condensation
Woo love
Woo choices
Fuck condemnation
Woo love
Woo chance
Woo fortune favors all the brave
Woo sun
Woo condensation
Woo love

//

Woo Love QR Code

Camille Ora-Nicole

For Woo Love

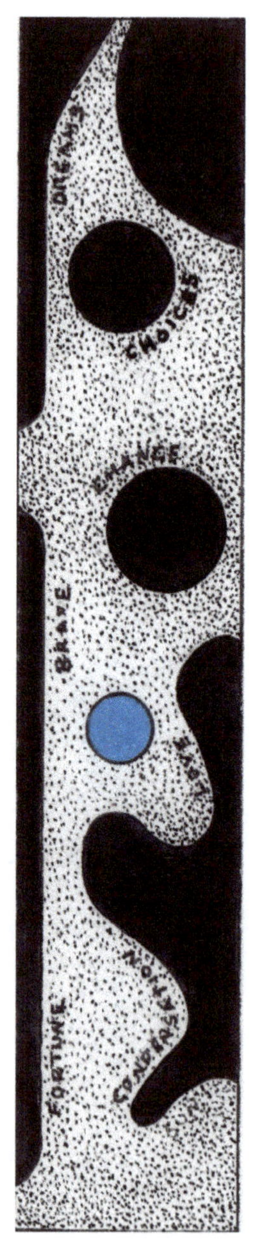

Delicious

I ate myself
I fixate

It's delicious

I could eat you too
What a state to be in

Trance—delicious

What a world
Unto ourselves

Staying in heaven
To avoid hell—

//

Camille Ora-Nicole

For Delicious

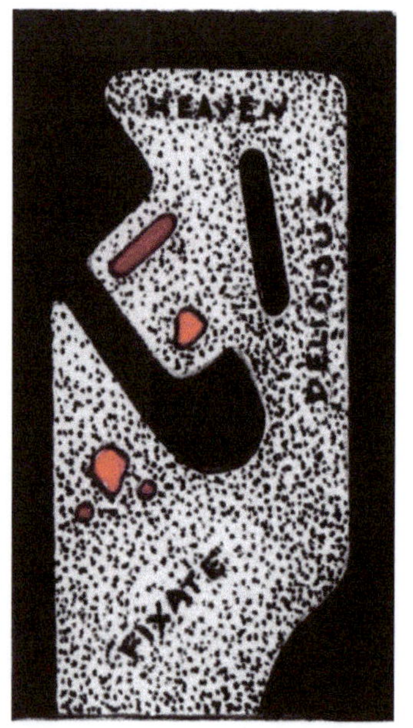

Grapes of Wrath

My cheeks are as red as
The wine I can't drink,
Trying to bring your passion
Into fruition—

The grapes of wrath are
Delicious, but they make me sick.
I'm not paid enough to
Puke for you.
I'm not paid enough to
Worship you.
I'm not paid at all.

My lips are as red as the
Flaming bullshit I tell,
Trying to make you content with
Your own ideas—

The grapes of wrath are
Delicious, but they make me sick.
I'm not paid enough to
Praise your prose
I have no desire
To be your parent.

//

Camille Ora-Nicole

For Grapes of Wrath

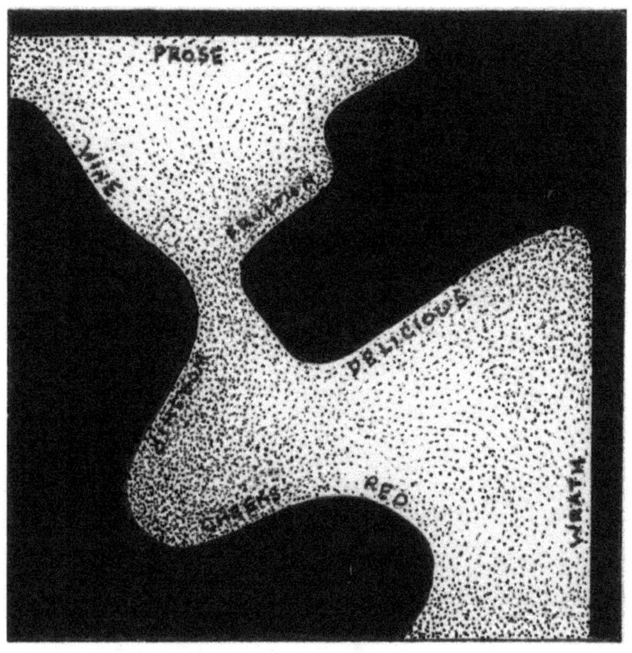

Check on Me

I haven't slept in two weeks
Why has nobody checked on me?
Does my tone mask it all so sweetly
Why has nobody checked on me?
I know the exact tone of blue at dawn
Why has nobody checked on me?
There's not a single lightbulb in my mind on
Why has nobody checked on me?

I've laughed with TikTok humans more than real ones
Why has nobody checked on me?
I only know the Story ongoings of all my friends
Why has nobody checked on me?
My mind is racing so hard it's leaving skid marks
On the inside of my skull
And all my dreams are tsunamis
With no one bothering to save me
Why won't nobody check on me?

Maybe because I won't pick up a phone either
Maybe cuz I'm still learning empathy, especially for me
Maybe cuz I say all the wrong things
My filter is broken, either blocking too much
Or cracked or frayed, either way it's fucked, out of whack
Call it Tierra, though I wish it were more colorful

I haven't slept in two weeks
Why has nobody checked on me?
Does my tone mask it all so sweetly
Why has nobody checked on me?
I know the exact tone of blue at dawn
Why has nobody checked on me?
There's not a single lightbulb in my mind on
Why has nobody checked on me?

I've got a new project to distract from my old ones
Why has nobody checked on me?
They make me excited, then make me nauseated
Why has nobody checked on me?
I'm climbing up fake cliffs for a burst of endorphins
Why has nobody checked on me?
And to stop myself from jumping off real ones
Why has nobody checked on me?
I'm eating donuts, I don't even like donuts
Why has nobody checked on me?
Watched Girl, Interrupted, got the warm fuzzies
Why has nobody checked on me?
Don't know if the fuzz in my head is long COVID,
Dementia or stress but it's starting to blend
And all my dreams are tsunamis
With no one trying to save me
Why has nobody checked on me?

Maybe it's because I never say a thing
Maybe it's because I never check on nobody
Maybe it's because I don't say enough
Maybe it's because I laugh more than I weep
Maybe it's because I'm too far away
And I never travel, don't take a break
Maybe it's because I pretend I'm a brute
Maybe it's because I act too steady too fall

Maybe next time someone calls,
I will tell the truth.

//

Give Thanks

Give thanks
That this day
And this place
Is just imagination

If this place is make-believe
I can also make believe
Make this life-shit just for me
I am that I am

If this place ain't fitting you
Get new shoes, yeah go bespoke
Don't mind none that old folk spoke
You are that you are

Give thanks
That this day
And this place
Is just imagination

My reality's between my waist and my thighs
My reality's the galaxies in my eyes
My reality has got you cotton-candy spun
My reality blooms in full color when you come

My reality's between your waist and your thighs
My reality's the galaxies in your eyes
My reality has got me cotton-candy spun
My reality blooms in full color when I come

Give thanks
That this day
And this place
Is just imagination

//

Monologue

Her body is not our art; her bosom, it's
    A weeded valley of rebus, not
    Ever rendered accurately, turquoise
    But grey, choppy but smooth; and her mood, it's
Mercurial—she smiles while she rages. She's not
    Wanting of machinations, not aching for lapis
    Enamel to boost her worth. Her beauty, it's
Not our art, it's actually
    Our ruler, a master hypnotist shrouded in cerulean—

//

Words Like Petals

Words like petals fall one by one from my mouth,
delicately aspiring to inspire love, even while a
flurry of jabs may be best in this case,
straight to the point, straight to the head

—*I love you*—

not "you glow in the sun," not "your smile drowns sorrow," just

—*I love you, do you love me too?*—

no dreams of tsunamis, no timid embraces just

—*I love you, do you love me too? I love you regardless, my
shirt is yours*—

//

For Macro Micro Atomic

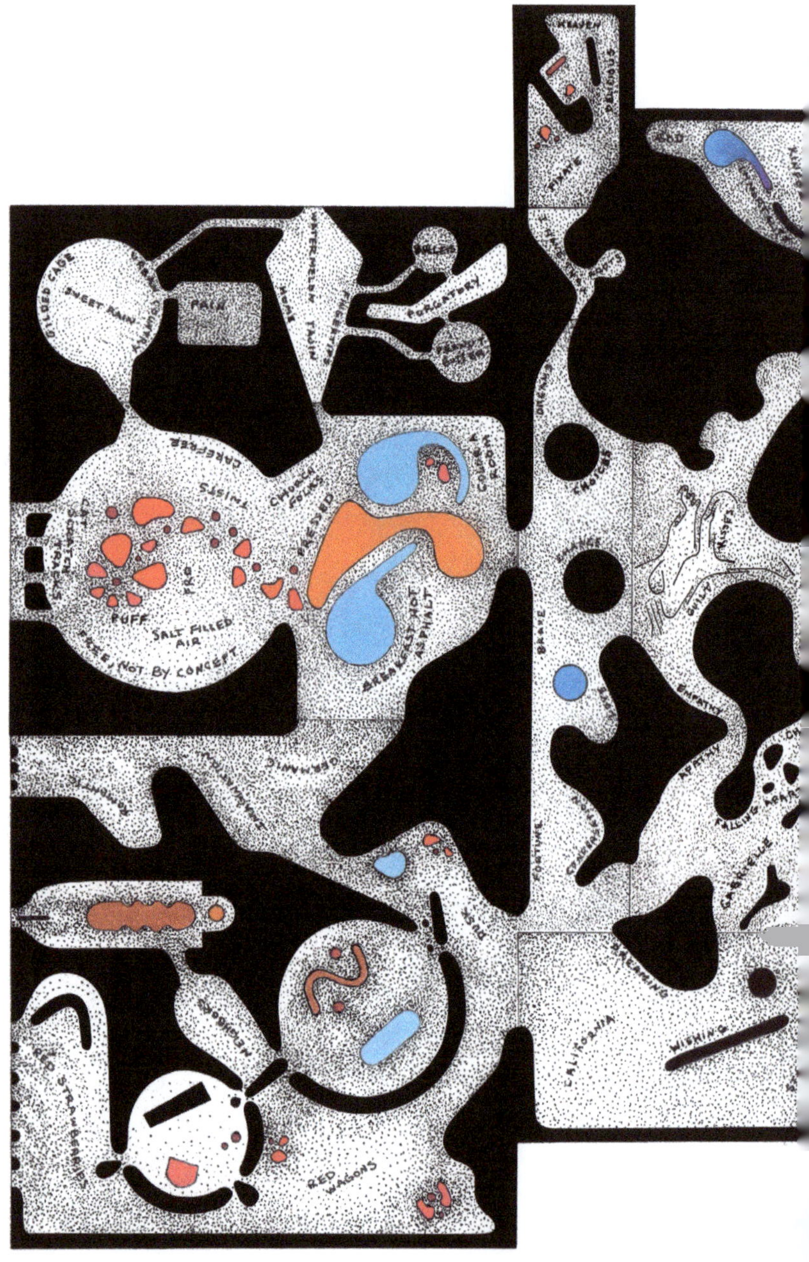

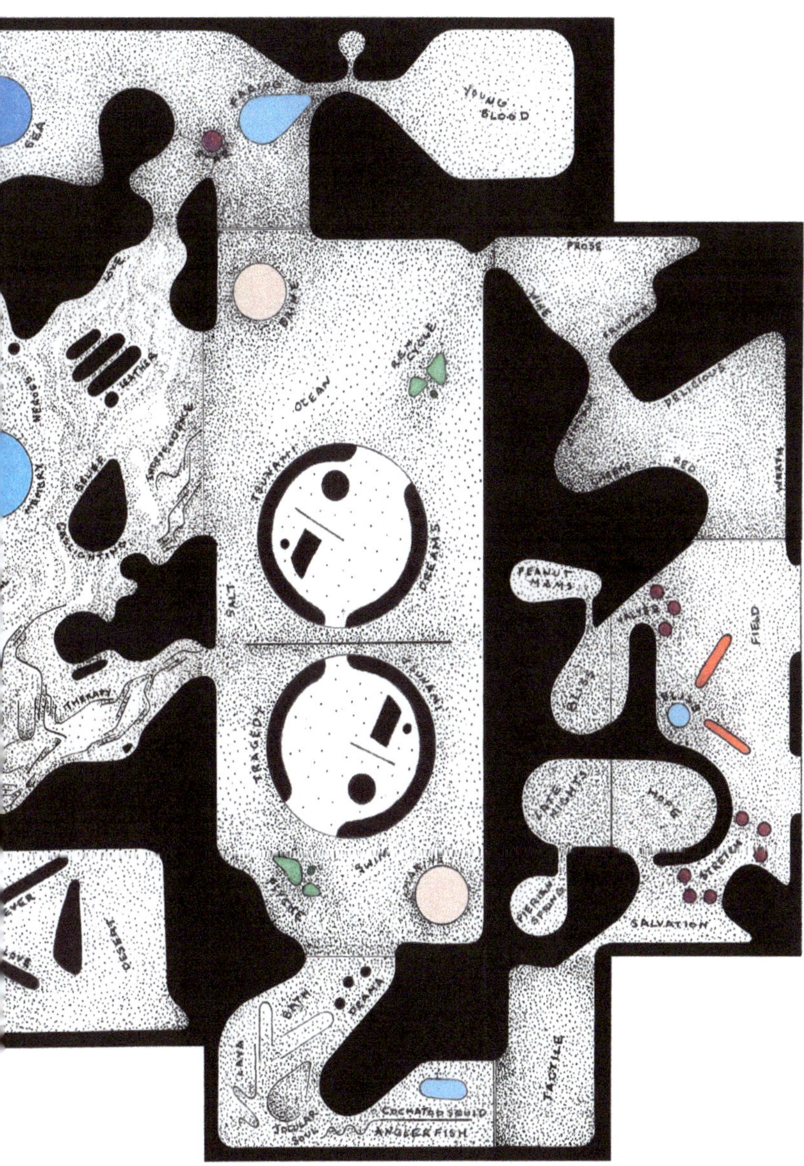

SEA
FRIEND
YOUNG BLOOD
PROSE
HEATHER
LOVE
SOUR
NORTHERNER
OCEAN
RED CLIQUE
DELICIOUS
LEAF
RED
WREATH
SAVORY
COLONIZING
TOURNAMENT
DREAMS
SALT
PEANUT M&Ms
VALUER
FIELD
BLISS
THERAPY
TRAGEDY
UMAMI
LATE NIGHTS
HOPE
SWING
PIZZA
STRETCH
FRENCH
FEVER
DESERT
LOVE
SALVATION
BATH
DEATH
TACTILE
CREMATED SQUID
ANGLERFISH

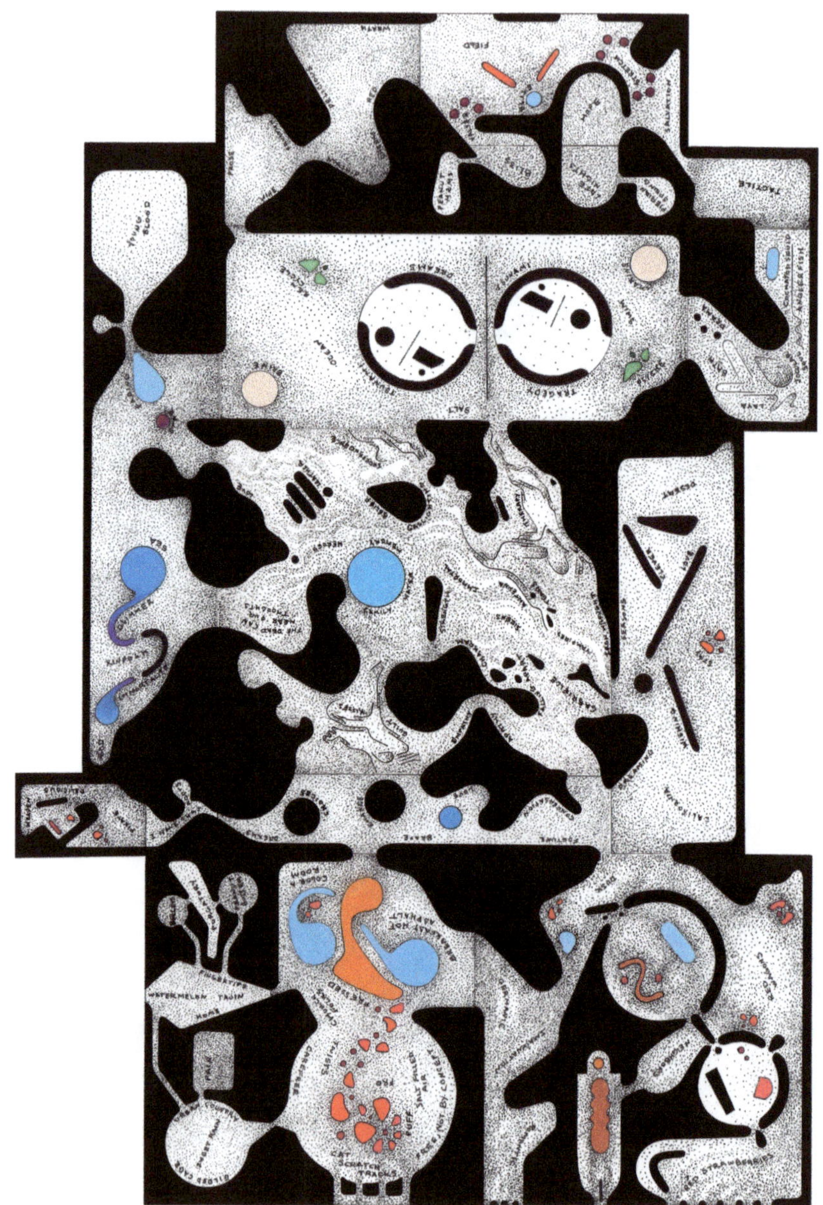

www.ingramcontent.com/pod-product-compliance
Lightning Source LLC
Chambersburg PA
CBHW041335120726
48005CB00014B/2268